HOMES
Like Mine

Marie-Therese Miller

Special thanks to Stephanie Garrity, Executive Director of Rainbows for All Children

Lerner Publications ◆ Minneapolis

To my family, wherever we are together, I am home.

Lerner Publications Company
An imprint of Lerner Publishing Group, Inc.
241 First Avenue North
Minneapolis, MN 55401 USA

For reading levels and more information, look up this title at www.lernerbooks.com.

Main body text set in Mikado a.
Typeface provided by HVD Fonts.

Editor: Allison Juda **Designer:** Emily Harris
Lerner team: Martha Kranes

OurFamilyWizard is proud to offer the Many Ways series. Since 2001, OurFamilyWizard has been dedicated to supporting communication between parents who are raising kids from separate homes. Over the years, the understanding of what a family looks like has changed. But no matter a family's shape or size, the meaning of family has always remained rooted in love and respect. We hope these books help children learn the many different ways to be.

Library of Congress Cataloging-in-Publication Data

Names: Miller, Marie-Therese, author.
Title: Homes like mine / Marie-Therese Miller.
Description: Minneapolis : Lerner Publications, [2021] | Series: Many ways | Includes bibliographical references and index. | Audience: Ages 5–9 | Audience: Grades 2–3 | Summary: "There are many different kinds of homes for the many different kinds of families. Discover the different homes that are a perfect fit from apartments, to single-family homes, to mobile homes, and more"– Provided by publisher.
Identifiers: LCCN 2019046319 (print) | LCCN 2019046320 (ebook) | ISBN 9781541598041 (library binding) | ISBN 9781728400150 (ebook)
Subjects: LCSH: Dwellings—Juvenile literature.
Classification: LCC GT172 .M55 2021 (print) | LCC GT172 (ebook) | DDC 392.3/6—dc23

LC record available at https://lccn.loc.gov/2019046319
LC ebook record available at https://lccn.loc.gov/2019046320

Manufactured in the United States of America
1-47995-48673-2/7/2020

Table of Contents

All Kinds of Homes

Homes keep families **HAPPY** and **SAFE**.

What kind of **HOME** do you live in?

Some families live in a **HOUSE**.

One family usually lives in this kind of home.

An **APARTMENT** is a home inside a larger building.

Families in apartments can have many NEIGHBORS in the building.

Some homes can be **MOVED** to different places.

But these homes usually stay at **MOBILE HOME** parks.

Sometimes a **FAMILY** might not have a home.

They could stay in **SHELTERS** for a while. Or they might live with **RELATIVES**.

TOWNHOUSES are homes that are attached to one another.

They **SHARE** walls with their neighbors.

There are homes for **MILITARY** families.

They can live on a military **BASE** or **POST**.

Some children have **TWO HOMES.**

They spend some time at one parent's home and some time at the other parent's home.

People live on floating **HOUSEBOATS** and in **TREE HOUSES** too.

People even live in **LIGHTHOUSES** that shine bright lights to keep ships safe.

There are many different kinds of **HOMES**. Homes give families a place to share time **TOGETHER**.

Glossary

base: an area where members of the military live and train

lighthouse: a tower in or near a large body of water with a flashing light at the top that helps keep ships away from danger

military: having to do with soldiers or the armed forces

neighbor: a person who lives next to you or nearby

post: an area where soldiers in the military live and train

relative: a family member

shelter: a place where people without homes can stay

Further Reading

Brundle, Joanna. *Homes around the World.* New York: Smartbook Media, 2019.

Dinmont, Kerry. *Homes Past and Present.* Minneapolis: Lerner Publications, 2019.

Houses around the World
https://www.kidcyber.com.au/houses-around-the-world

Miller, Marie-Therese. *Families Like Mine.* Minneapolis: Lerner Publications, 2021.

O'Connell, Eleanor. *Homes around the World.* New York: Gareth Stevens, 2017.

Types of Homes
https://kidspicturedictionary.com/english-through-pictures/place
-english-through-pictures/types-of-housing-and-communities/

Index

Photo Acknowledgments

Image credits: 10'000 Hours/DigitalVision/Getty Images, p. 4; Monkey Business Images/Shutterstock.com, p. 5; Mableen/E+/Getty Images, p. 6; Ariel Skelley/DigitalVision/Getty Images, p. 7; stevegeer/E+/Getty Images, p. 8; xavierarnau/E+/Getty Images, p. 9; David Cowlard/Construction Photography/Avalon/Getty Images, p. 10; Nancy Nehring/Moment Mobile/Getty Images, p. 11; Wendy Maeda/The Boston Globe/Getty Images, p. 12; SDI Productions/E+/Getty Images, p. 13; blackestockphoto/E+/Getty Images, p. 14; Grace Cary/Moment/Getty Images, p. 15; U.S. Army Garrison-Hawaii/United States Department of Defense, pp. 16, 17; Caiaimage/Sam Edwards/Getty Images, p. 18; fizkes/Shutterstock.com, p. 19; Alex Levine/500px/Getty Images, p. 20; Aneese/iStock/Getty Images, p. 21; Sidekick/Getty Images, p. 22.

Cover: Photo by Sgt. 1st Class Doug Sample/United States Department of Defense (top left); RiverNorthPhotography/iStock/Getty Images (top right); deberarr/iStock/Getty Images (bottom left); Mark-W-R/iStock/Getty Images (bottom right).